Amazing Animal
Tool-Users and
Tool-Makers

by Leon Gray

Raintree is an imprint of Capstone Global Library Limited, a company incorporated in England and Wales having its registered office at 7 Pilgrim Street, London EC4V 6LB Registered company number 6695582

www.raintree.co.uk
myorders@raintree.co.uk

ISBN: 978-1-4747-0219-5 (HB)
ISBN: 978-1-4747-0225-6

For Brown Bear Books Ltd:
Text: Leon Gray
Editor: Tim Harris
Picture Researcher: Clare Newman
Designer: Karen Perry
Design Manager: Keith Davis
Production Director: Alastair Gourlay
Editorial Director: Lindsey Lowe
Children's Publisher: Anne O'Daly

British Library Cataloguing in Publication Data
A full catalogue record for this book is available from the British Library.

Acknowledgements
1, Sergey Uryadnikov /Shutterstock; 4, John Michael Evan Potter/Shutterstock; 5t, Evron Photo/Shutterstock; 5b, Maryna Pleshkun/Shutterstock; 5br, Chris Gomersall/Alamy; 6t, Sharon Day/Shutterstock; 6-7, Pete Oxford/Minden Pictures/FLPA; 7tl, Jean-Edouard Rozey/Shutterstock; 7tr, Charles Heyser/Shutterstock; 7cr, Jono Lethbridge; 8, DMV Photos/Shutterstock; 8t, Gerry Ellis/Minden Pictures/FLPA; 9b, Dr Clive Bromhall/Getty Images; 10, Hal Beral/Corbis; 11t, Maryna Pleshkun/Shutterstock; 11b, Doc White/Nature PL; 12, Anup Shah/Minden Pictures/FLPA; 13t, Jurgen & Christine Sohns/FLPA; 13b, Sergey Uryadnikov/Shutterstock; 14, Roland Seitre/Nature PL; 15t, Chris Gomersall/Alamy; 15b, Jerry Morse/Dreamstime; 16t, Hugh Lansdown/Shutterstock; 16b, Kajornyot/iStock/Thinkstock; 16-17, E. D. Torial/Alamy; 17tr, Andrea Izzotti/Shutterstock; 18, Nick Haynes; 19t, Wong Wean/Shutterstock; 19b, Nazrul Islam/Photoshot; 20, David Tipling/FLPA; 21t. Konrad Wothe/Minden Pictures/FLPA; 21b, Ingo Arndt/Minden Pictures/FLPA; 22, Fiona Ayerst/Shutterstock; 23t, Colin Marshall/FLPA; 23b, Alex Mustard/Nature PL; 24-25, David Psborn/Shutterstock; 25tl, Outdoorsman/Shutterstock; 25tr, Sorbis/Shutterstock; 26, Max Allen/Shutterstock; 27t, Lukas Blazek/Dreamstime; 27b, Sylvain Cordier/FLPA; 28, Arto Hakola/Shutterstock; 29t, Bruce MacQueen/Shutterstock; 29b, Biosphoto/Superstock.
t=top, c=centre, b=bottom, l=left, r=right

All artworks © Brown Bear Books Ltd
Brown Bear Books has made every attempt to contact the copyright holder.
If anyone has any information please contact licensing@brownbearbooks.co.uk

Some words are shown in bold, **like this**. You can find out what they mean by looking at the glossary.

Printed in China
20 19 18 17 16
10 9 8 7 6 5 4 3 2 1

Using lures

Some creatures use **lures** to attract **prey**. Alligators cover their head with sticks and weeds. If a bird lands to take a stick for its nest, the alligator grabs it. Herons sometimes drop bread into water. When fish come to the food, the birds seize them.

A human angler does something similar when fishing with a rod and line. The angler puts a fly, or **bait**, on the end of the fishing line to attract the fish.

COPYCAT

People use a stone or wood **pestle** to crush and grind tough food, such as peppercorns in a bowl. This way of making tough food edible is much the sam smashi a **mollu**

WOW

Magpies are the only birds that can recognise their reflection. In an experiment scientists stuck a coloured dot on a magpie's beak and put the bird in front of a mirror. The magpie tried to remove the dot, showing that it recognised its own reflection.

Guide for readers

Throughout this book, special feature boxes accompany the main text, captioned photographs and illustrations. COPYCAT boxes highlight some of the ways in which people have been inspired by the animal world. WOW boxes provide incredible facts and figures about different animals.

Tools for feeding

One of the main reasons animals use tools is to help them reach food. Tasty insects sometimes hide deep in holes in tree trunks. Shellfish are protected by hard shells. Animals have found ways to overcome these problems.

Sticks and stones

Chimpanzees and some crows use sticks or thin twigs to get insect **larvae** out of burrows in wood. The animals choose a stick that is just the right size to fit the hole. They may even bend a twig to fit. If an orangutan cannot reach fruit in a tree, it sometimes uses a stick to pull the fruit closer.

Capuchin monkeys, chimps and Egyptian vultures smash open tough nuts, fruits and eggs with stones. Sea otters break open hard shells on rocks. Some crows drop nuts in front of cars to break them open.

Birds called jays hide nuts to eat later. They make signs to remind them where they left the food.

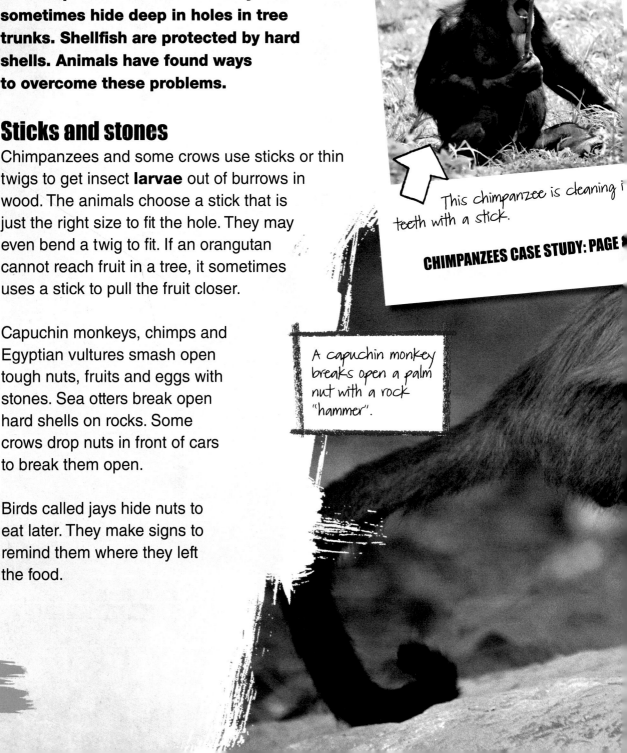

This chimpanzee is cleaning i teeth with a stick.

CHIMPANZEES CASE STUDY: PAGE

A capuchin monkey breaks open a palm nut with a rock "hammer".

Sea otters break open crabs on rocks to get at the meat inside.

SEA OTTERS CASE STUDY: PAGE 10

Orangutans use a stick to pull fruit and other food towards them.

ORANGUTANS CASE STUDY: PAGE 12

Jays are crows that bury nuts to eat later. They leave signs to show where they stored the nuts.

CROWS CASE STUDY: PAGE 14

Chimpanzees

Chimpanzees are some of the most intelligent animals of all. They live in groups in forests in tropical Africa. Chimps have a varied diet, but much of their favourite food is difficult to reach or hard to break open. They use tools to help them.

Life in the trees

Chimpanzees spend much of their time high up in trees. At night they sleep in nests of leaves. During the day they swing from branch to branch as they search for food. Chimps eat fruit, leaves, nuts, honey, insects called termites and the larvae of other insects. They complete their diet with birds' eggs and the remains of dead animals. Sometimes chimps form hunting groups to chase and kill monkeys for food.

Chimps use different tools to help them eat and drink. They use stones to break open hard nuts. They put the nuts on a flat stone surface and smash a rock down on them to reach the **edible** inside of the nuts. They scrunch up leaves and use them as sponges to soak up water to drink.

A baby chimp rides on its mother's back for the first few months of its life.

WOW

Chimpanzee mothers usually give birth to one baby. Mother chimps give their young food, warmth and protection. They also teach them skills, including how to use sticks to get food.

Small and large sticks

Chimps use sticks and twigs in different ways. They poke long, thin sticks into the nests of termites. The insects cling to the stick, and the chimp laps them up when it pulls the stick out. Chimpanzees bend twigs into hooks and use them to dig insect larvae out of the **crevices** in tree trunks. Chimps use larger sticks to smash open beehives and collect the honey inside.

A chimp uses a stone to break open tough-shelled nuts.

Sea otters

Sea otters live along the Pacific coast of North America. These animals use stone tools to break open shellfish such as clams, mussels and abalone.

Life in the water

Sea otters spend almost all of their lives in the ocean. They are well-adapted to their watery **habitat**. Sea otters have webbed feet and a rudder-like tail to help them swim in strong ocean currents. Their thick fur keeps them warm and waterproof. When an otter dives, it closes its nostrils and ears to keep out the water. Sea otters even sleep in water.

A sea otter eats the soft meat of a clam after breaking open the hard shell.

Hard-shelled food

Sea otters eat shellfish, sea urchins and crabs. Most of their prey is protected by a hard shell, so the otters use tools to get their food. They use stones to knock sea creatures off rocks and to smash them open.

Smash and grab

The sea otter dives down to the bottom of the ocean. It picks up a stone and a shellfish, such as a clam. Then it swims back to the surface and floats on its back. The otter holds the stone on its chest and smashes the shellfish against it. When the shell breaks open, the otter eats the soft meat inside. After it has eaten, the sea otter washes its fur to keep it clean and waterproof.

COPYCAT

People use a stone or wood **pestle** to crush and grind tough food, such as peppercorns in a bowl. This way of making tough food edible is much the same as a sea otter smashing a rock against a **mollusc** shell.

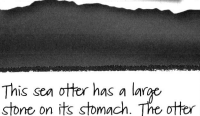

This sea otter has a large stone on its stomach. The otter uses it to break open its food.

Orangutans

The orangutan is an unmistakable sight in the rainforests of Borneo and Sumatra. These apes have long, orange hair and long arms and legs. They spend most of their life in trees.

A female orangutan and her baby rest in a nest of branches and leaves.

Person of the forest

The name orangutan means "person of the forest" in Malay, the native language of Borneo and Sumatra. The apes use their long arms to swing between the branches. The biggest males have an arm span of up to 2 metres (7 feet). Orangutans sleep high up in trees. They make nests from leafy branches and cover the nests with large leaves. The leaves shade the animals from bright sunlight and act like umbrellas to keep out the rain.

This orangutan is using a stick to find insect larvae in a hole inside a fallen tree.

Many uses for sticks

Orangutans use tools to help them eat. They use long sticks to "fish" for out-of-reach fruits. They use sticks to break open fruits with hard husks.

Orangutans use tools in other ways too. They use sticks to measure the depth of a river to make sure it is safe to cross. They use leafy branches as scratching sticks and to swat away annoying insects.

WOW

Male orangutans live alone. They make howling calls as they move through the rainforest. These calls tell other orangutans to stay away. The apes put leaves in front of their mouths when they call. This alters the sound of their calls.

Crows

There are more than 120 different kinds of birds in the crow family. They include jays, magpies and ravens. Crows live in most habitats, from tropical rainforests to city parks. They use a variety of tools to help them find food.

A New Caledonian crow probes for grubs with a stick.

Food for thought

Carrion crows live in cities. They have developed an amazing way to break open hard nuts. The birds drop nuts onto a pedestrian crossing and wait for cars to drive over and crack the hard shells. The crows wait until the traffic lights turn red and the cars stop. Only then do they fly down to pick up the nuts in safety.

New Caledonian crows make tools from twigs and leaves. They bend and shape them into hooks. Then they poke the hooks into holes in tree bark to find insect larvae.

Jay signposts

When there is too much food to eat, jays and other crows often hide some of it. They return to eat months later when other food is scarce. Jays choose their hiding places carefully. They bury food next to posts or trees. This helps the birds remember where the food is. Jays sometimes make their own "signposts" from rolled-up leaves. They put these in the ground by the buried nuts.

WOW

Magpies are the only birds that can recognise their reflection. In an experiment scientists stuck a coloured dot on a magpie's beak and put the bird in front of a mirror. The magpie tried to remove the dot, showing that it recognised its own reflection.

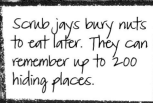

Scrub jays bury nuts to eat later. They can remember up to 200 hiding places.

Tools for building

Many animals build shelters to protect themselves from the weather or from predators. Some animals use tools to make their structures warmer or stronger.

Building a nest

Some **mammals** build a shelter for themselves and their young. Chimps and orangutans make nests in the treetops to sleep. But the best-known nest-builders are birds.

Birds build nests out of twigs, leaves and moss. A nest is a good place to lay eggs and protect young chicks. Tits line their nests with feathers. This keeps the nests warm. Tailorbirds stitch their nests with plant **fibres** or sticky spider silk. This makes their nests stronger.

Bowerbirds use tools to attract a mate. They build structures called **bowers**. The birds decorate the bowers with colourful flowers and shiny insect wings. Female bowerbirds are drawn to the brightest bowers.

Some animals use tools to hide from **predators**. The veined octopus collects coconut shells from the seafloor. It hides under a shell when a predator comes near.

Male bowerbirds use coloured objects to brighten their bowers.

**BOWERBIRDS
CASE STUDY: PAGE 20**

Tailorbirds are named for their special weaving skills.

**TAILORBIRDS
CASE STUDY: PAGE 18**

Female red ruffed lemurs build twig nests for their young. The lemurs line the nests with their own fur.

Veined octopuses carry shells and coconuts to sheltered places.

VEINED OCTOPUSES CASE STUDY: PAGE 22

Tailorbirds

Tailorbirds are small birds that live in tropical parts of Asia and Africa. They are named for the way they sew leaves together to build their nests.

A tailorbird has sewn this nest together with silk from a spider's web.

Sewing leaves

A female tailorbird starts to build her nest in a small tree. She chooses a large green leaf about 1 metre (39 inches) above the ground. The bird uses her long, pointed beak to pierce holes on each edge of the leaf. Then she sews the edges together using spider's **silk** or the fibres from a plant. She pulls the thread through the holes on opposite sides of the leaf and ties a knot to stop the thread from pulling through. She repeats this for every hole to form a pouch. This pouch will support and shelter the nest inside.

A place to lay eggs

The nest is made inside the pouch. It is woven from fine strands of grass. The male tailorbird helps the female line the nest with feathers and other soft plant material.

When the birds have finished building, the female lays up to five eggs. The eggs are blue and brown and speckled. They hatch after about two weeks, and both parents look after the chicks. The parents collect insects, berries and tiny seeds to feed the chicks. The chicks are usually ready to leave the nest after about three weeks.

COPYCAT

Engineers sometimes use rivets to hold plates of metal together. To prevent the rivets from falling out, each one has thick ends. These are like the knots that a female tailorbird ties at the end of each thread to keep it from dropping out of a leaf.

A tailorbird with a length of plant fibre. The bird will use this to tie two sides of a leaf together.

Bowerbirds

Bowerbirds live in the rainforests of Australia and South-east Asia. A male bowerbird uses a variety of tools to build an enclosure, or bower. If a female bird likes the bower, she will mate with him.

Shapes and sizes

Males build bowers of different shapes and sizes. Some build a simple platform of leaves, stones and twigs. Others build an "avenue" bower. They push two rows of sticks into the ground to form a domed tunnel. Another design is a circular bower built around a small tree. The male arranges sticks around the tree and uses twigs, moss and leaves to make the roof. When it is finished, the bower looks like a hut with a thatched roof.

This bowerbird is decorating its bower with blue objects.

Once the male has built a bower, he decorates it with brightly coloured objects. They include berries, feathers, flowers and shiny shells and insect wings. Sometimes the bird collects human rubbish, including coloured pens, shiny coins and broken bits of glass. The male bowerbird spends hours arranging the objects around the bower.

Choosing a mate

A female bowerbird often visits the bowers of several males before picking a mate. The males sing and strut around their bowers while the female checks them out. She chooses the male with the most attractive bower. Young males that have not learned how to make a good bower will not attract a mate.

After she has mated, the female leaves to build her own nest and lay her eggs. She raises her chicks without help from the male.

WOW

Satin bowerbirds paint the walls of the bower with chewed-up berries. Male golden bowerbirds line the walls with tiny flowers (see below).

Bowerbirds often arrange the objects they collect by colour.

V in d octopus s

The veined octopus is one of the only invertebrates (animals without a backbone) that uses tools. It picks up clams and coconut shells from the ocean floor and turns them into hiding places.

Living on the seafloor

The veined octopus is a small, soft-bodied sea creature. It has a small body, just 8 centimetres (3 in) across, and eight arms. Each arm is about 15 centimetres (6 in) long. The arms are covered with suction cups that the animal uses to catch its prey. It eats shrimp, small crabs and clams.

The octopus lives in tropical waters in the Pacific and Indian oceans. It lives in the shallow waters near the coast. When it is not swimming, the animal sometimes buries its body in the sandy seafloor. It leaves just its eyes uncovered. This is not the best place to hide. A passing predator would quickly spot it.

A veined octopus hides in an old shell. This animal lives in water up to 45 metres (148 ft) deep.

Predators sometimes attack veined octopuses while they are moving shells.

Shell shield

To protect itself from predators, the octopus picks up a clam shell or half a coconut shell from the seafloor. It stretches its arms over the shell and carries it to a safer place. If a predator comes near, the octopus turns over its shell and hides underneath. If the octopus has both halves of a shell, it squeezes between them to hide. It keeps very still until the predator has passed.

WOW

Veined octopuses once just used clam shells as hiding places. Now they also use coconut shells because people have thrown so many of them into the ocean. The creatures are also called coconut octopuses.

Tools for attack

Many predators use speed and power to overcome other animals. Other hunters lie in wait for passing prey. A few predators use tools to trap or lure their victims.

Blocking the way

American badgers block the burrows of their prey. They fill the entrances of ground squirrel burrows with stones and dirt. Then the badgers dig their victims out of the ground. The ground squirrel cannot escape from its burrow, so it is easy to catch. Some insects have a similar method. Predatory wasps use grains of sand to trap burrowing insects, keeping them as a "larder" to eat later.

Animal lures

Some alligators use sticks and weeds to trap birds. The alligators balance the plant material on their head and swim near the water's surface. The sticks tempt birds looking for nest materials, and the alligators grab them.

Birds also use tools to catch their own prey. Herons drop pieces of food into ponds to attract hungry fish. Burrowing owls collect animal dung. The dung attracts dung beetles, which the owls eat.

Green herons drop bread into water to attract fish. The herons then eat the fish.

American badgers block the holes of prairie dogs and other prey with stones.

AMERICAN BADGERS CASE STUDY: PAGE 26

Some alligators put lures on their head to attract prey.

ALLIGATORS CASE STUDY: PAGE 28

American Badgers

The American badger lives on the grasslands, or prairies, of North America. It digs in the ground in search of burrowing mammals, such as ground squirrels and pocket gophers.

American badgers dig for prairie dogs, gophers and other animals that live underground.

The American badger is built for digging. It has a short, stocky body and powerful front legs. Each front paw has sharp claws 5 centimetres (2 in) long. The claws easily scrape through the sandy prairie soils. Badgers dig burrows for shelter. They also dig to hunt their prey.

Underground larder
The badger's main food is small, burrowing mammals, such as ground squirrels, pocket gophers and prairie dogs. These animals live in burrows that usually have more than one entrance.

The badger blocks most of the entrances to the burrows with loose soil and and stones. Just one entrance is left uncovered. Then the badger waits to catch its prey as it tries to escape through the only exit.

Hunting pairs

American badgers and coyotes often hunt together. As the badger digs, the coyote pounces on any prey that escapes. The badger catches any animals that stay in the burrow, hiding from the coyote.

WOW

Honey badgers are close relatives of American badgers. Honey badgers live on grasslands in Africa. They use logs as bridges to get to out-of-reach food. They also move pieces of wood onto fences and other obstacles so they can climb over. Captive honey badgers have even been filmed unlocking bolted gates!

An American badger blocks the entrance to its prey's burrow.

Alligators

The American alligator lives in the wetlands of the southern United States. This deadly predator is one of the few **reptiles** that uses hunting lures as tools to capture its prey.

An American alligator has grabbed a waterbird that came too close.

Deadly predators

American alligators are top predators of the swamps and marshes of the United States. They lie in wait for their prey for hours on end. American alligators eat a range of food, from insects and fish to turtles, snakes and small mammals. In fact, American alligators will eat almost anything that fits into their enormous, gaping mouths.

The American alligator collects sticks and small branches and uses them as lures to attract birds. The alligator swims near the water's surface with the sticks balanced on its snout.

If a wading bird, such as a snowy egret, flies down to pick up the sticks, the alligator strikes. Alligators only use lures during the nesting season. At this time wading birds are looking for material to build their nests.

Mugger crocodile

American alligators are not the only reptiles to use sticks as lures. The mugger crocodile from the marshes of South Asia uses sticks in a similar way.

WOW

Wading birds, such as herons (see below), nest in areas with high populations of alligators. Scientists think birds choose to nest there because the alligators drive away other predators, such as snakes.

This alligator is almost hidden by the weeds and plant stems on its head.

Glossary

ape large primate that lacks a tail. Chimpanzees, gibbons, gorillas and orangutans are apes.

bait food used to attract fish and other animals so that they can be caught

bowers structure built by a male bowerbird to attract females to mate

crevices cracks and holes in the trunk of a tree

edible something that can be eaten without harming the animal eating it

fibres thin, but often strong, threads produced by a plant or spider

habitats natural homes of animals or plants

larvae young form of animals, such as insects, jellyfish or amphibians

lures things to attract and catch animals

mammals animals with warm blood and fur. Female mammals produce milk to feed their young.

molluscs varied group of animals. Some, such as clams, mussels and abalone, are protected by hard shells. Others, including cuttlefish and octopuses, have no such protection.

pestle tool for grinding food

predator animal that hunts and eats other animals

prey animal that is hunted and eaten by other animals

reptiles cold-blooded animals with scaly skin, such as alligators, lizards and snakes

silk strong, fine fibre produced by spiders and many insects

tropical warm regions to the north and south of the Equator

Read more

Alligators and Crocodiles (Amazing Animals), Sally Morgan (Franklin Watts, 2013).

Animals that Dig (Adapted to Survive), Angela Royston (Raintree, 2014).

Animals that Fly (Adapted to Survive), Angela Royston (Raintree, 2014).

Chimpanzees (Animal Families), John Woodward (Wayland, 2014).

Internet sites

BBC Nature
Information on tool use by capuchin monkeys, chimpanzees, orangutans, jays and elephants.
www.bbc.co.uk/nature/adaptations/Tool_use_by_animals

National Wildlife Federation
Lots of information about sea otters.
www.nwf.org/Kids/Ranger-Rick/Animals/Mammals/Sea-Otters.aspx

Listverse: 10 Surprising Ways Animals Use Tools
Examples of tool-using animals, including gorillas and herons.
listverse.com/2012/12/29/10-surprising-ways-animals-use-tools

Index